ZOOM FOR TEACHERS

The Easy and Practical Guide to Effective Online Teaching.

Prepare, Manage, and Run your Virtual Classroom Smoothly with Zoom

EMILY ROSE JOHNSON

Table of Contents

Introduction

Due to the challenges posed by the global epidemic disease, remote meetings have become more necessary. This explains the recent increase in usage of the Zoom application by teachers around the world working from home to reduce the spread of the virus.

Zoom allows individuals to meet and work together in a 'face-to-face' manner effectively when meeting in person is not possible. That makes the meeting much more remote, which is essential to help users feel connected and stay connected. The number of Zoom users this year has risen rapidly.

Zoom allows teachers to create lessons and organize the different training activities by enabling the various applications, such as sharing multimedia materials, chats, discussion forums and social networking and virtual classrooms.

As a teacher, whether you or your learners have a condition that prevents you from meeting face to face, Zoom will help to keep your class running. Concurrent online class meetings, where everybody is expected to attend a Zoom group, are one way to build interaction while students are far. Still, Zoom may also be used to help special education and learning situations. Zoom may be used on any device and even workstation phones, allowing students to connect with the team meeting in many ways. You can find tips on planning for your Zoom meetings in this book, gathering students with the conversation, screen editing, polling, non-verbal reviews and breakdown rooms, and supplying your community with open online learning sessions, as well as resources for different teaching scenarios.

The system offers some basic features: it is accessible through the Internet; it bases the learning paths on the multimedia material (text, audio and video); it continuously monitors activities and includes tests to evaluate results; it allows interaction between students and teachers.

When it comes to online instruction, there are critical pieces that must be maintained across all courses. Student surveys about online courses typically show a correlation between poor teaching and learning and the online instructor's ability to communicate. Instructors have frequently noticed when they provide consistent due dates, expectations, rubrics, and strategies throughout a course, the students learn more and leave them more positive feedback.

If the success of online teaching in colleges and universities can teach us anything, once the online learning starts and the students feel comfortable, it would be the growth of distance learning, and would eventually become an indispensable part of any good educational program. Online learning is here to stay. Those who want to stay at the top of this profession will learn, grow, and adapt their instruction. It is up to current teachers to learn from the lessons of non-traditional instructions and transform online learning into the schools of the future.

Without further ado let's get started.

Chapter 1: Getting Started, Basics of Zoom, How Does Zoom Work, Setting Up a Virtual Classroom

What is Zoom?

Zoom is a video conferencing tool that is cloud-based and allows you to host one-on-one virtual meetings or virtual team meetings effortlessly. With powerful video, audio, and collaboration features, this distant communication tool links inaccessible team members with each other.

Some vital features of zoom include:

- Hosting video webinars

- HD video chat and conferencing

- Instant messaging

- Screen sharing and collaborative whiteboards

- Virtual backgrounds for video calls

- Audio conferencing using Voice over Internet Protocol (VOLP)

Basics of Zoom

Individuals love utilizing Zoom since its configuration works for them 99.99% of the time, with no requirement for IT support. The effortlessness of the structure causes clients to feel like they are in charge of their gatherings.

Profile Page

At the top left corner of the dashboard is a profile link where you have access to your profile details, and you can manage features like changing of profile pictures, getting your meeting ID, your sign-in email, user type, meeting capacity, language, and the rest.

Meeting Page

The meeting page is the next, which is right below the profile page, at the top left-hand corner of your dashboard.

From this page, you can do a whole lot of things like:

1. Scheduling a New Meeting

2. Access Previous Meetings

3. Access a Personal Meeting Room.

A personal meeting room is reserved explicitly for you; this is where you have your meeting ID and invite link among others.

4. Meeting Template

Meeting Template is a place where you can customize your meeting by choosing a session, and can also edit and save it as a template for future use.

Get Training

Get Training is a dedicated page for training.

Webinar Page

What is a Zoom video webinar? It merely enables you to host a broad audience with audio, video and screen sharing for nothing less than a hundred participants and ten thousand attendees.

Recording Page

The **Recording Page** is a page dedicated to your recordings, either locally or by cloud.

13

Settings Page

You will see a lot to work while on this page. You can set or reset your meeting, recording and telephone settings.

How Does Zoom Work

Zoom's principle administration is video correspondences. The interface is straightforward enough for anybody to see how to utilize it in only a couple of moments. The application configuration includes a video **upfront** style approach, with a solitary control bar on the base.

The Zoom meeting control bar highlights straightforward symbols that speak to the receiver control, camera use, members, talk, screen sharing, recording, and response. Zoom keeps up an oversimplified and natural interface, and a considerable lot of these symbols drill down to get to more profound degrees of control. In the engine, Zoom offers numerous video conferencing highlights that its rivals don't. Hence, Zoom has gotten the most love for power clients who host loads of online gatherings. Clients frequently pick Zoom for its significant rundown of highlights; however, the genuine excellence of Zoom is its dependability.

Setting Up a Virtual Classroom

The first step to take if you utilize Android or iOS gadgets is getting the app or proceeding to the official website to utilize the program. Select **Sign up** to start creating a free profile for yourself. Users can sign up through the use of email addresses or utilizing their social media accounts. Whenever you finish the app and verify your profile, the platform will download the application to your device automatically.

Let the prompt guide you through the installation process of the app and log into the app with your details. Although you do not have to open an account before attending a meeting with the platform, it is advisable to create one if you want to enjoy all of the extended attributes of the platform, which includes owning a profile or hosting a meeting.

The program comes with different types of plans, and the basic plan is free for everyone but comes with restrictions. The basic plan limits your meeting time to forty minutes and allows up to one hundred attendants on a maximum. After forty minutes, it is easy to rejoin or restart the meeting almost immediately. Users also have the opportunity to buy a subscription plan that eradicates its limits and includes other important attributes that can be of great advantage to your organization or business, as the cloud storage of your records and advanced controls for your meetings.

How to Register

After downloading the app, the next task to perform is to register for the service. You can perform the task with your smartphone or personal computer, but we will firstly talk about the web service.

Navigate to the page for sign up, and you will find different options that you can utilize to create an account. Input your email address into the text field with the name email. The platform will demand a work email, but you should not worry about that because your email is enough, and will function properly in the place of a work email.

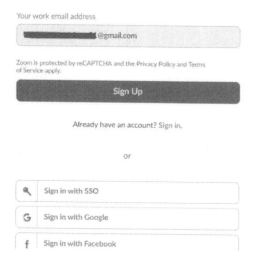

The only risk attached to utilizing a personal email is that the app sometimes thinks that users with specific email domains work for the same organization, and that is the privacy issue associated with the platform. However, you should know that the platform does not include some popular email domains such as Yahoo and Gmail in the generalization.

Users can also create a profile by selecting the **login with Google or Facebook** button on the login page, which will, in turn, download the program's application to your computer with just one click.

After inputting your email, the platform will send you an authorization email. Select the **activate control key** in the email to activate your account. You can also copy and paste the link to your browser to get your account activated.

When the page launches on your browser, input your names and passkey.

You can invite other attendants on the following page to create a free profile through the use of an email.

The platform will provide a link to the meeting URL for you, and you can select the **Begin Meeting** control key to start it. After performing that task, it will start downloading the app on your device. Let the prompt guide you through the installation process.

After installing the app, there will be several buttons to help you navigate through the platform. You will find buttons like the **Sign In** or **Attend a Meeting**. You can start a test meeting immediately by tapping **Login**.

The following screen comes with text fields for your email and pass-key, the information required for you to log onto the platform.

After the login process, ensure that you are on your **Home** tab, then select the **New Meeting** control key on your application, and it will start the meeting.

If you sign up for the platform through your mobile application, it has a related method of setting up and installing the web concept.

Get the Android or iOS app and launch it. It will display several options for you to navigate through different sections of the platform, which includes the **Sign In** or **Sign Up** control keys to get started. Select **Sign Up**.

The following screen comes with text fields for you to input your names, email, and a box to check for the terms of services agreement. Select **Sign Up**, and the platform will send an authorization email for you to activate your account.

Select the **Activate** control key provided in the email sent to you or copy and paste the URL included in the email into your browser.

The platform will ask you to finish the same steps required for you to create a profile through your browser.

After that, it will take you to the screen containing the **Begin Meeting** control key and your meeting URL. Feel free to select your desired choice, and it will take you to a waiting room for testing meetings.

You can start a meeting by clicking the **Sign In** control key below your visual display. Input your login details and select the **Sign In** control key on the following page. It will launch your text meeting in the application.

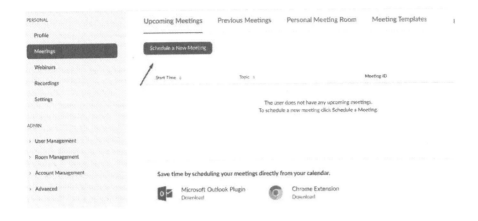

Invite Participants

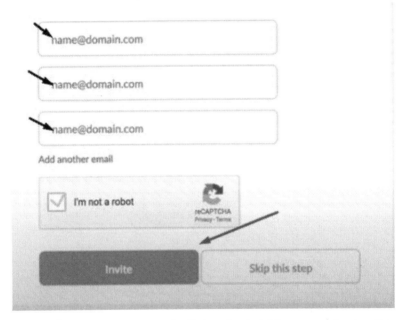

After creating your account, it is straightforward to invite different participants to your meeting. The platform allows users to invite attendants to a meeting in various ways. If you utilize mobile or desktop applications, select the tab for

Meetings and follow the instructions below:

If you select the **Copy Invitation** control key while utilizing your desktop application, it will copy a message containing several important information. They include your meeting identity, URL, and mobile details to your clipboard, where you can drop a message or email.

Whenever you select the **Send Invite** control key on your mobile application, it will display three alternative options. Send a message which lets users send a **Text the Meeting URL** to another person. Send an email for launching an email, including the details of your meeting and copy it to the clipboard. It copies information like the identity and URL of your meeting to your mobile's clipboard.

Users also have the option of inviting several other participants while in use:

If you utilize a desktop application, navigate to your toolbar by moving the mouse inside the window for your meetings and select the **Invite** control key. After performing that task, the platform will launch a window for you to invite your contacts and will send information through email on how to participate in the meeting. Then copy the URL of your meeting to your clipboard.

If you utilize a mobile application, select **Participants**, and click on the **Invite** control key beneath your following visual display. After performing that task, the platform will let you send an invitation through email, through text messages and perform several other tasks.

Downloading the Zoom App

Signing up for an account is pretty easy, as is setting up your own account, and it is also free; click on **Sign Up**.

It is a free icon at the top right hand of your dashboard.

You can sign up with either your work or business email or a Yahoo or Hotmail account.

Sign Up Free

Your work email address

Zoom is protected by reCAPTCHA and the Privacy Policy and Terms of Service apply.

Sign Up

Already have an account? Sign in.

Or you can sign in with either your Google email or Facebook account as well.

So, I'm going to sign up with Google because it's the easiest way to sign up. So, choose the email that you want to use, then all you need to do is click **Create Account**.

Now, welcome to your Zoom dashboard. This is where you can manage your recordings. You can see previous meetings as well as the meetings that are coming up and create templates.

Download Zoom to Your Computer

After getting familiar with the Zoom dashboard, the next practical step is to download the Zoom to your computer to begin using it.

There are practically two ways of downloading Zoom to your computer.

Scroll down the page, under download, click on **Meetings Client**, and download.

OR

Go to **Host a Meeting** at the top right-hand corner of your dashboard.

Click on any of the options among the trio of **With Video Off**, **With Video On**, or **Screen Share Only**.

SCHEDULE A MEETING   JOIN A MEETING   HOST A MEETING ▾

Then, it will lead you to this page, and then you are done with the download.

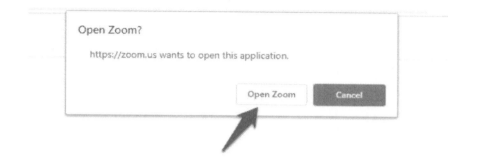

Chapter 2: Should I Use Zoom Meetings Or Zoom Video Webinars To Host A Class? (Difference between Zoom Meetings Plans)

How to Select Zoom Plans

Zoom enables a one-on-one discussion time that can grow into group calls, vocations, training workshops and websites for internal and external audiences, and international video conferences with up to 1,000 participants, and up to 49 screen videos. Freebies allow unlimited meetings one by one but limit the group time to 40 minutes and 100 participants. The paid plan starts at $ 15 per month per host.

It is vital to know that the solution offers four different pricing structures, ranging from **Basic** to **Enterprise**. Whether you intend to use the basic software, is based on what is best for you.

Zoom Basic

The Zoom basic is the most common price scale on the app, which makes a lot of sense, given that it is free of any cost. This level provides an endless one-on-one session, but video conferencing is restricted to 40 minutes, with more than three people (you could always initiate session). If you are planning on using it once in a while to chat with family or friends, then its basic feature will suffice.

Here is a summary of its features:

- The ability to host meetings with up to 100 participants (This could be more if you are using a paid version).

- Allow students to virtually raise a hand as a signal to the teacher that they have a question.

- Helps teachers explain concepts on a virtual whiteboard.

- The ability for teachers/trainers to share their screen /slides with students in the form of PowerPoint presentations, videos, folders, websites, online stores, etc.

- Teachers can block unwanted sounds/noise from participants.

- Participants/students can be blocked or removed during the ongoing teaching session.

- Participants/students can chat amongst themselves.

- Teachers can split students into break out classes using Zoom's random tool, or by manually grouping the class into smaller groups.

Zoom Pro

The Zoom Pro option is perfect if you are working with a small group or are planning to run prolonged video calls frequently. This package enables consumers to create IDs for ongoing sessions, has the capacity to retain recorded sessions in the server, and has advanced usage reports, in addition to extending the community meeting duration from 40 minutes to 24 hours.

Zoom Business

A price model to facilitate collaboration between small and medium-sized enterprises requires at least ten guests. But what you will get as an exchange on all invitations is corporate brand identity, committed customer service, and more functionalities like auto-generated transcription.

Zoom Enterprise

The Zoom Enterprises category is for large enterprises and needs a minimum of 100 guests during sign-up. Enterprise gives satisfaction, such as limitless data cloud storage, a committed customer success manager, and the ability to host a single call for 500 people.

When you want to turn to a new plan, you should; you will not be locked into one plan permanently. Here is a simple method to assist you in downgrading or upgrading your Zoom subscription plan at any given time.

The video conference network also provides products expressly tailored for students, telemedicine companies, and software engineers in addition to these price points. Each of these companies comes with its own attributes and client support structures.

Once you have selected a package, installing it on your PC, or on your phone or tablet is easy. Zoom is available in the Google Play Store and Apple Store for Android, iPhone, and iPad devices, respectively.

If you are going to use your machine, you will need to go to and access the official site of Zoom. The method will be subtly different according to the type of device you are using:

- You will need to learn how to install Zoom on your computer.

- You will need to learn how to install Zoom on Mac PC.

You do not even need a login to participate in Zoom conferences, but if you intend to broadcast, schedule, and manage your own calls, you have to create an account if you are planning to utilize the system frequently. Whether for a personal or for business purpose, we suggest that you first download the software and register for a Zoom profile.

Chapter 3: How Do I Take Classroom Attendance and Verify Those Who Are Present?

Manage Attendants

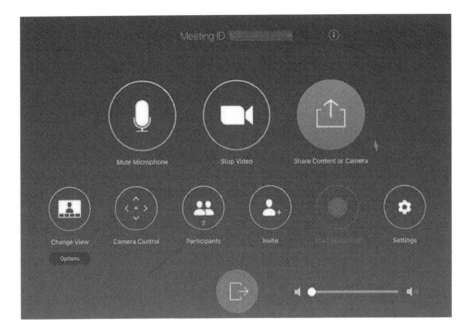

You could control the attendants in a video conversation if you created it. Every attendant in the group can distribute different materials like videos and so on, by default. You can also limit the number of people who can distribute files while the conversation is on utilizing the webinar platform. Before you start managing individuals in a video interaction, it is important to understand the order of attendants. They are:

- You

- The admin (If that is not you)

- Contact information without names

- Muted and Un-muted attendants

Only the admins can utilize the below attributes:

- Letting the attendants' record locally

- Changing the status of an attendant from a member to co-host or host

- Authorizing the waiting room

- Managing the attendants

To go through the attendant's list, select **Manage Attendants** inside the controls. Select the menu that drops down, which you will find around the attendant's list, or select **pop out** to divide the list through the page for the meetings:

Hover on an attendant and select **More** for the below actions:

- **Chat**: Launch the page for the chat to get your

messages to the admin.

- **Halt Video**: It can stop the attendant's video so that they cannot start or launch their camera. Sometimes the attendant may not start their camera, but it will display the start control key.

- **Designate Host**: You can utilize it to modify the status of people by making them the host. You can only have one.

- **Designate Co-host**: It can also make the attendant a co-host, and there is no limited number for co-hosts.

- **Enable Record**: It can let an individual stop or start recording the interaction locally. Attendants cannot cloud records.

- **Rename**: It gives users the ability to modify the name of people that other attendants can see. You can utilize this feature in only current meetings.

Note: To modify your name that you can see, hover on it in the list of attendants and select **Rename**. You must know that this change is not permanent, and if you want a permanent change, you should modify it in the profile. You can also place people in the waiting room, while you utilize the available time to make preparations for the meeting. If you are hosting, then you should allow the waiting room so that it can appear for you to use it.

- **On-hold**: If you do not allow the waiting room, it will display the on-hold option where you can put people on hold.

- **Remove**: It helps the host remove attendants when they complete the project or at any time they desire. You should know that any participant that you remove cannot rejoin until you allow them again. It gives you access to allow and disallow the above options beneath the list of attendants.

- **Invite**: It lets you invite other individuals.

- **Mute and Un-Mute All**: It gives you the power to un-mute or mute individuals in the current group.

- **Let Attendants Un-Mute Themselves**: It gives attendants the power to un-mute themselves to share an opinion.

- **Let Attendants Rename Themselves**: It gives the people the power to modify their identity that others can see whenever they desire.

- **Lock Meeting**: You can use this attribute to lock every other attendant out of the meeting.

- **Join Windows For A Meeting**: Merge the list of attendants with the original window for the interaction. Utilize this alternative if you divide the list of attendants from the initial one.

- To stop attendants from sharing the visuals, navigate to the settings. Select the arrow close to the **Share** screen and tap **Advanced Sharing**.

Chapter 4: How Do I Ensure My Classroom Is Secure?

Before you continue utilizing the platform for your business and other purposes, you must understand the privacy and security issues of the platform.

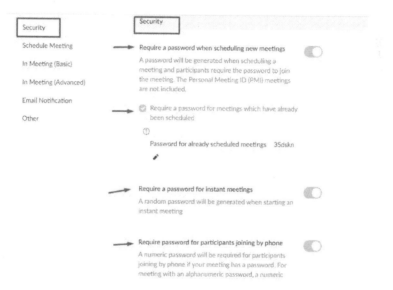

The platform claims to utilize the end-to-end concept of encryption, and that means that it should not have access to video and audio communications. However, the reverse is the case, and the platform can access, host a video meeting, an interaction, and serve several other purposes at any given time and location. It is a flaw that can jeopardize important information distributed through the platform.

There have been lots of reports about data privacy issues associated with the platform. There are several tasks you can perform on the service, which includes a record of meetings, documents, and generated texts while the meeting was going on. You should also know that organizations with paid accounts have lots of control over their workers. They can join any meeting hosted by any worker and also keep track of their data without permission or knowledge.

Lastly, another major concern is zoom-bombing. It is the location where users get access to meetings and try to interfere by displaying forbidden materials in the meeting. The producers of the platform found a method of combating that problem by ensuring that each user meets the password requirements by default.

Best Practices in Securing Your Zoom Classroom

We want to share with our respected educational organizations, the best practices that can be implemented, to ensure that your school uses attraction services in a way that best contributes to the safety and privacy of students, teachers, and administrators who are your users. Better approaches help you find and maintain a safe and secure learning area for your users, businesses, and schools. But many of these methods can also be applied in colleges.

Be Sure To Get Parental Consent

Remember that the obligation to obtain parental consent when necessary, as it applies to students and their information, rests with our educational companies. Zoom trusts that you get parental consent for your children to use Zoom Services. Your organization must be able to demonstrate compliance with the parental consent requirements under the COPPA and other applicable laws.

Account Creation Monitoring

Class students in institutions not up to the age of 16, should not visit *www.zoom.us* to create an account. They should only be permitted to attend Zoom sessions where participants (not separate account holders through the school account) and children cannot create an account under the **Zoom Terms of Use.**

The account manager (teachers) should provide security and confidential information about meetings and passwords for student users' appointments to ensure that the school can maintain and manage the student meeting experience.

MSI Option

- Account administrators can use this tool with user settings that are suitable for Zoom Desktop's main settings, and ensure that these settings apply to all downloads in your school account.

- Allow users to only participate in organizational accounts meetings.

- If you provide student equipment, you can lock the Zoom client so that users can only attend meetings from your school account provided and can only be used for school-related purposes.

- It requires an account login to attend a meeting.

- If you use a school email address, to enable this setting, users will need to register securely to attend a school meeting held at the school and ensure that all attendees are present and identified.

Zoom Registration Panel

Meeting guests can ensure that only registered and recognized attendees can attend the meeting.

Meeting Security and Management

The chairman of the meeting has a variety of controls that they can use to secure their meeting. By default, Zoom has enabled the queue, required a password for meetings, and set the screen sharing mode to **Only Hosting,** for a more secure meeting.

- **Prevent Participants From Sharing Screen**: By

default, only hosts can prevent screen sharing from interfering. If you choose to allow others to share, the host can click the arrow next to the **Share** box, and click **Advanced Sharing**. Who can share? Select **All Participants** and close the window.

- **Standby:** By default, the standby is enabled, which allows the host to control the participant when attending the meeting. Once at the meeting, click **Manage Meeting Attendees** and **Accept** to allow attendees to attend the meeting.

- **Meeting Password:** Zoom requires a default training password as the default. When you create a meeting, the password is embedded in the meeting/website links. When you enter the session ID manually, the user is always prompted for a password.

- **Lock Meeting:** When you are in a meeting, click **Participants** at the bottom of the Zoom window. In the attendee's popup, you will see a button that says, **Lock Fund.** When you lock a meeting, new participants cannot join, even if they have a meeting ID and password.

- **To Expel a Participant:** You can still use the mouse over the participant's name in the participant's menu. Some options appear, such as **Delete**. Click here to kick the participant out of the meeting. They cannot re-enter if you click **Lock Session.**

- **Pending Participant:** If you need private time, you can pause participants. The participant's video and audio connections are temporarily removed. Click the participant's video thumbnail, and select *Start Participant on Hold* to enable this feature.

- **Video Off:** Instructors can turn off the participant's video and ask you to start the participant's video. This allows mentors to block unwanted, annoying, or inappropriate gestures in the video.

- **Mute Participants Or Mute All:** Mentors can rotate participants or mute anyone. This allows mentors to avoid unwanted, annoying, or inappropriate noise from the meeting.

Turn Off Private Chat

To ensure that students focus on the lessons available, meeting organizers can limit students' ability to talk to each other during the meeting or disable the internal discussion of the meeting in its entirety.

Disable Group Messaging Between Accounts or Restrict Student Chats

You can limit the use of groups and chats (outside the

meeting) or restrict the conversation to certain contacts, such as mentors or counselors, by limiting students' ability to send or share personal information to other students in public. This can be done with chat groups.

Zoom Data Breach and Security Accusations

The recent accusations of data breach and infiltration in Zoom has led many people to switch to other services. There were reports of bugs in the URL generation that lets hackers eavesdrop on private conversations, security issues in the Windows 10 build, and phone data being sent to Facebook even with the absence of a social media account. Upon the revelation of these accusations, Zoom ensured that they were implementing end-to-end encryption that provided critical security. As expected, Zoom tried to clean up its mess, as much as it could. To make up for these mistakes, the platform will no longer serve meeting ID numbers in the address bars. Moreover, an additional security tab can be accessed by hosts and participants to provide adequate security settings. Also, the service has stepped up to provide secure geofencing measures to provide the option of entering and exiting out of particular data center regions. These norms were recently established, and the service is taking further measures to make the platform more secure and private for use.

While using this service, you can take a few measures to ensure further security while attending a call.

- **Create a Password:** This is the simplest way to make sure that no unknown user infiltrates your meeting and space. It takes no time at all to create a password and forward it to your participants.

- **Do Not Allow Participants to Share their Screen:** Unless it is extremely necessary, turn off the option that allows your invitees to share their screen.

- **Enable the Waiting Room Feature:** While this is not entirely related to privacy, it does bring a sense of controlled security for the overall session to the host.

- **Remove Users That Cause Nuisance:** As we learned, you can remove a particular user by accessing the **More** option and removing them from the meeting.

- **Do Not Generate your Own ID:** Let Zoom generate an ID for you. There is a higher chance of any known or unknown user deciphering your ID through several means (it can be shared publicly by mistake, or you could be hacked). Every time you schedule a meeting, let Zoom generate the ID for you.

- **Lock your Meeting:** Once all your participants are present in the room, lock the meeting to avoid infiltration. To do this, go to **Manage Participants**, tap on **More**, and select **Lock**. Make sure that you follow this procedure after all your expected participants have arrived in the room.

- **Check for Updates Regularly:** This is probably the most important tip of all. As we know, Zoom is working to provide safer access to its service with enhanced security features and tools that ensure minimal chances of data leaks. Zoom will likely add bug-fixes, or deploy certain security measures with each update. Keep on checking for updates now and again. To do this, open the desktop app, click on your profile that is located on the top-right corner of the home page, and tap on **Check for Updates**.

Chapter 5: How Do I See All My Students on Video and Combined Calls?

Zoom is identical to Skype and Google Hangouts, a video-chatting app. It can be used to attend online courses, remotely visit friends and family, and even join social activities such as birthday parties. For teachers, the free version of Zoom offers a range of helpful features, including the ability to organize meetings of up to 100 people, and encourage students to send wordless signs to the instructor that they have a problem, and work on projects by annotating documents on the screens of other students. Plus, Zoom also eliminated the 40-minute free accounts limit for K-12 students.

An updated version of Zoom, however, preferably controlled by the school or district management department, will include additional tools and power, including logging features, an admin portal, controlled domains, single sign-on, and more. It's critical that you contact your school or district administrator before you step in with some new tech device. You will also need to ensure that parents agree to use Zoom and are well aware of how it can be used and what security you have for children.

Audio Settings

First, you will tweak the audio settings. To begin with, find the **Join Audio** at the bottom-left corner of the window, and click the arrow beside it. Click on **Audio Settings** from the dropdown menu.

A **Settings** window will pop up, which will look like this.

You can always access this window by clicking on the setting icon at the top right part of the screen.

- Once the window pops up, click on the dropdown list located on the right side of **Test Speaker** and select the speaker you prefer. You can either choose your headphone jack, your device's speaker, or any other speaker that is linked externally. We would recommend that you wear headphones, as it will block out the background noise and keep your meeting private if other people are around.

- Next, you should check the microphone quality. Click on the dropdown menu on the right side of **Test Mic**. Depending on the microphone device you are using, select the relevant option. If you have an external microphone connected to your system, the list will display the name. If not, select **Same as system** to use the device's microphone.

- Then, you will check the input level of your microphone and voice quality. Start talking and view the slider besides **Input Level**, as it transitions from red to green. Your audio is stable if you are in the green zone (not too slow and not too loud). Check the box beside **Automatically adjust microphone volume** to make it easier.

- Leave the other settings as they are. You can probably check the box that says **Join audio by computer when joining a meeting** to access the same setup as soon as you join a call.

Video Settings

Now, we will tweak the video settings. Click on **Video** located above **Audio** in the left panel.

The video settings box will look like this.

- As soon as you click on **Video**, a box appears with a message saying, '*Zoom would like to access the camera.*' Click on **OK**. The black box in this picture will display what is seen by your front-facing camera. This is how the other participants will see you during the call. You can adjust your position and device to provide a clear view.

- If you have other devices or webcams attached externally to your video interface, select the device from the dropdown menu beside **Camera**. Leave the other settings as they are and exit the box.

Stop Video Option

Once your audio and video settings are in place, you are good to go. Close the setting page and click on the **New Meeting** button to start a meeting. If you need the call to be just audio, you can select the **Stop Video** option on the bottom-left corner of the window, as you access to the meeting.

Combined Calls

More than one person may attend meetings. A public officer may want to co-manage the meeting with the leader, or a team with more than one leader may prefer each of the co-owners rather than choosing one person over another. Whatever your circumstances, you can call Zoom and entrust the management to more than one person.

To use shared hosting tools, you must first enable it in the Zoom meeting settings. Find the **Meeting tab**, and select the **Shared Host option**. Then, when you start the meeting wait for your co-host to join in and add the person by clicking on the three dots that appear when you hover over their video box. In addition, you can go to the **Participants** window, select **Manage Participants**. Move the mouse cursor over the name of the co-owner and select **More** to find the option **Make Co-Owner**.

Requirements: To use shared hosting, you need a Pro, Business, Education, or API Affiliate account with Zoom, and you need to work on MacOS, Windows, Android, or iOS (Not Linux or web). If this option does not appear, ask your account administrator to enable the settings on the **Meeting tab** for sharing the rights.

Chat Options

Access the **Chat** option on the bottom of the main window. It will open a popup window. This will allow you to write comments and send messages during the meeting. You can also upload files or photos from your device, Google Drive, or Dropbox by clicking on the file icon.

This is particularly convenient if you want to discuss certain specifications during the meeting, such as presentations, reports, or diagrams. In case you wish to send a private message to a participant you will need to click on **Everyone,** and select from the list the person that you wish to contact.

Importance of Scheduling

Scheduling is important, even if you are working remotely. In fact, it might be more important if you tend to procrastinate or have a habit of delaying submissions and assignments. With proper scheduling, you can respect deadlines and get work on time. Treat your home as your workplace. When it comes to video conferences, schedule your calls beforehand, and inform the required participants about the meeting details. This should include the meeting ID or password (to enter the meeting), the topic of discussion, time, date, and duration of the meeting. Having prior knowledge of the forum will ensure that your participants are thoroughly prepared and ready to engage in the conference actively.

Even though it might seem unimportant, scheduling does help keep track of your operations, especially if you need to consult your team occasionally. Set reminders to alert you an hour before your meeting. You do not want to be late for a meeting that you host.

Setting goals while working from home, without physical assistance from your team, is tough. When you want to continue your business, you need to consult and gel with your team constantly. This is not entirely possible while working virtually. To be as effective as possible, you should set certain goals. Whether it relates to your year-end turnover or establishing communication within your team, a set of objectives will help you when you are working at a distance. Set goals, host a meeting, and communicate with your team over a video conference. You may need to spend hours in the planning stages before you begin communicating with your employees.

Trim these goals into processes and tasks, and assign them to relevant employees and departments. Try to simplify the tasks as much as possible to maintain coordination among your team members. Keep track of the tasks that you have assigned to your team members and stay connected virtually at all times. Ensure clarity between your team members and conduct **after-action** reviews once the deadlines are reached.

This practice might take up to 90 days for it to become routine, but once you do, you will close in on your target. Conduct trial sessions in between to keep the workflow stable. Since there is a lack of constant communication and observation, ensuring productivity can be difficult. Hold regular review meetings and convey your expectations about intermediate milestones, despite a lack of face-to-face communication.

The point is, you may need to learn to micro-manage to be a true leader with virtual meetings.

Chapter 6: How Can I Ensure I Sound My Best During My Online Event?

Make Proper Use of the Microphone

This step is a very important step because it ensures that everyone participating in a Zoom meeting or lecture is carried along. People participating in a meeting may also have to make use of the **Chat** functionality to pass a request to the person chairing a meeting to get them unmuted so that they can pass information to the other participants. Most video conferencing rooms have a provision for a microphone. A microphone ensures that all sounds from one part of the conferencing room that is directly in contact with the microphone are heard in other parts of the room. These include side commenting, whispering, sneezing, eating, page-turning, tapping a pencil, a sound made while eating, etc.

Zoom Meeting Etiquettes

1. Stay in an appropriate environment with a professional background.

2. Dress appropriately.

3. Mute your microphone until when ready to use it.

4. Avoid eating during a meeting session.

5. Make sure you have a good internet connection.

6. Silence cellphones.

7. Have a pen and paper ready to take notes to avoid distractions.

If you are alone, this is less important, but wearing headphones with a microphone will give you a better sound because you are wearing headphones and using a microphone that is closer to you.

'Touch Up Your Appearance'

This additional beauty filter is useful when you are just out of bed and need to attend an important meeting. It provides a dewy and filtered touch-up to your face, offering a fresh look. At times, video calls can alter your look despite dressing up and wearing makeup. This is when the beauty feature can come in handy. It makes you look well-rested by smoothing your facial features.

To access this feature, tap the up arrow that is located next to the **Start Video** button and click on **Video Settings**. You will find **Touch up My Appearance** below **My Video**. Check the box, and you are good to go.

Dress for the Occasion

The dress is another significant aspect. It is better to clothe yourself absolutely; otherwise, as one CEO did, you could unintentionally show boxers underneath the suit and tie. Dress up with an emphasis on convenience, rather than sophistication, when in doubt. Video conferences can be pretty long, and the more comfortable you are in your clothes, the more attractive the opportunity.

Focus on the House Furniture

Furniture is essential, both when you are just a single participant, and when organizing a video conference for a group. The chair and table should be ergonomically set up to enable a natural, comfortable seating. In group settings, the focus should be on oval tables rather than the classic, long conference tables.

Invest in a Good Camera

Healthy hardware is an absolute **must** in all situations. Cameras that are built-in the laptops are a poor choice for video conferencing because they often ignore the accuracy of the recorded video and audio. Even the cheapest webcam will dramatically outperform those offers, allowing for a trouble-free conference. Ideally, you are going to want to look at business solutions designed specifically for video conferencing and delivering superior performance in all aspects.

Webcam does not ask you to drop 250 dollars on the most expensive webcam you can find. Many webcams can deliver the professional quality of video that makes Zoom's high-definition and high-quality video quality shine. A 720p (1280 rb720) camera would be adequate for this. To stop choppy footage, get one under this resolution, which can produce at least 20 frames per second. If you want to invest the gas, get one that will shoot up to 30 frames per second.

Get a camera with a highly sensitive autofocus and light correction capabilities to counter sudden movements and changes in lighting. It can be annoying to have to change your camera's focus manually, as participants watch your fingers fiddle around the lens.

Good Lighting is Important

Whatever the camera model you use, it is absolutely important to have good lighting. Poorly lighted spaces are the right way of hampering call quality and affecting your contact with others.

The Right Posture

Next are the finer details, such as keeping the proper posture. Slouching is out entirely, but the way you sit may impact the video conference quality. Try to maintain a stance that is upright but comfortable, which will provide excellent back support. Sitting in the wrong posture for a long period of time brings too much stress on the lower spine, leading to pain and back problems. Neither will it make the conference enjoyable anymore.

Make Eye Contact

Human beings are social creatures, and one aspect of the intricate network of relationships is posture. A further issue is eye contact. In general, try to stay focused on the partner and aim your camera to make eye contact, or be as close as possible to one. This will not only make you look focused and respectful but will also give the conversation a more professional, direct tone.

Chapter 7: How to Conduct a Class Discussion and Mute Audio, Disable Video, and Mute Everyone

Teachers use Zoom in various ways based on their abilities, the needs of their students, and the input from their districts. Here are a few different ways that teachers should use Zoom to know the distance:

Document the Lectures and Share Them: Since certain students may not have stable internet at home or share laptops with certain family members, asynchronous lessons through which students will access pre-recorded lessons with their own schedules, render distance learning more egalitarian. You will use Zoom's recording function to create video tutorials, and then share the videos with students for later viewing.

Teach the Lessons at Work: Synchronous or life lessons are an alternative for schools and districts that have addressed the technology connectivity problem. Teachers set up a daily Zoom class time and direct students by remote instructions.

Bureau Hours: Many instructors schedule daily **working hours**, encouraging students to come in and talk with the teachers and peers informally.

Circle Day, Day for Songs, or Days for 'Show and Telling': Teachers use the Zoom to provide cohesion and support for pre-K and grade school children. Little ones can't really stick out for long, for video conferencing, so they're loving a chance to see their friends, listen to a story, and show off their toys, pets, baby sisters, etc.

How to Mute and Unmute the Sound

You may be asked to turn off the microphone during the session until you have a question or comment. This helps to minimize audio feedback. To mute the sound, click the microphone icon in the lower-left corner of the menu bar.

Chat

The chat feature offers the ability to send a chat during a session. You can send a private conversation to a single person or a message to all the participants.

Click

Enter the message and press **Enter** on the keyboard to send. Messages are automatically sent to all participants. To send a message to an individual participant through a private conversation, click the drop-down menu, and select the person's name.

How to Attend a Class/Meeting

Join the Meeting URL

Progress to email, newsletters, calendar messages, or other communications that provide a link to a pre-arranged meetings and tap on the URL to join the Zoom meeting.

Participate Through the Desktop Application with a Meeting ID

- Open the Zoom desktop application.

- Click the **Home** button.

- Click **Join** and enter your ID and name.

Stay with Web Hosting/Browsers

By default, users now have to log in to their attraction account or create an attraction account when attending a web server meeting. An administrator or user can turn this off on their settings page.

There are three ways to turn on the audio when you are in a meeting:

1. Use computer audio (recommended).

2. Call a conference call from your conference bridge (paid bill).

3. Ask Zoom to call you by entering your phone number and the meeting will ring your phone (paid bill).

Do's and Do not's

Assuming that you are on a formal call, there are certain dos and do not's you should follow as an active participant.

Do's

- **Create an Appropriate Setup**: No one wants to look at a messy background when they are talking to you on a video call. Needless to say, a clean backdrop is mandatory to conduct any video call. After you clean your surroundings, start the video camera to test how your video call looks and to ensure that your backdrop is appropriate. Set the camera at an appropriate angle. Keep it at eye level to ensure that the other person can see you with ease. Ask family members or roommates to keep quiet until the video conference ends, or remove yourself from a noisy environment. Next, check the lighting. A backlight can be extremely uncomfortable and distracting for the other person. Stick to natural lighting or overhead lighting.

- **Pay Attention and Stay Focused:** Staying focused is necessary while on a video call because failing to do so can show a sincere lack of professionalism. Try not to send emails, look elsewhere, and do not check your phone. Many people have a habit of constantly looking at themselves on the screen. This shows a lack of attention to the other person and you could come across as self-centered. Even if you have to look away, communicate it to the person who is on the call with you and excuse yourself for a second. However, try not to do that in the first place. Since you are more visible on video conferences when compared to physical meetings, people will notice when you are distracted.

- **Mute The Call When The Other Person Is Speaking:** By muting a call, the other person can talk freely without being disturbed. This is particularly useful during group conference calls. Participants can become easily distracted due to unwanted noises in the background, which is why you should mute yourself when you are not speaking. Consider switching off your video too. If someone interrupts your call or if you need to tend to something, switching off your video is convenient. However, at times, the other person is unable to focus with switched-off video screens. Ask their permission first and act accordingly.

- **Be Courteous:** Needless to say, you should be courteous to the other callers and display basic manners while the call is ongoing. Introduce yourself and ask others for their names as well. Try to remember as many as you can and address them by their name whenever you can.

- **Understand the Difference between a Video Call and an Email:** Some people fail to understand the importance of a topic of discussion. At times, even if the topic could be successfully discussed over an e-mail or slack, they decide to host a video conference, which is, in fact, completely unnecessary. Know the difference and stick to an email and you will not waste anyone's time. However, if the subject is intense and needs a verbal explanation for full comprehension, do not hesitate to schedule a video conference.

- **Check your Internet Connection and Speed Beforehand:** Before starting or participating in a video call, make sure that your internet setup is adequate. Check the broadband connection and speed. Do a test video call with one of your close acquaintances to ensure the connection.

Do not's

- **Do Not Interrupt the Other Person:** Constant interruption is off-putting. Wait for your turn. You will know when it is your turn to speak. If there is something urgent or important that needs to be spoken, give a signal, and then speak. If your colleagues are planning to host these meetings constantly, work out a set of gestures for permission to speak or ask questions, like raising your hand. You can also use the chat options available in most of the video conferencing services to ask a question or insert a comment without interrupting the flow of the speaker.

- **Do Not Multitask:** As mentioned, do not cause any distractions during the video call. Multitasking is the worst form of distraction. Basically, eating, checking your phone, talking to someone else, etc., are major forms of distraction that should be avoided at all costs. Wait for the call to end, or excuse yourself if it is extremely important.

- **Do Not Look Messy or Sloppy:** Along with a clean backdrop, a clean appearance is also necessary during a video call, particularly during professional meetings. Dressing in your comfiest pajamas and sweatshirt is fine if you are attending a virtual family gathering, but with a professional call, you need to change to formal clothes, at least from the waist up if you are sitting through the entire call. Do not forget to neaten your hair. Dressing for your audience will leave an impression.

While conducting or participating in a video conference, agree on one language and stick to it. This is specifically necessary if your video call involves people from all around the globe or for bilingual participants.

Chapter 8: How Do I Share My Screen And Contents During My Webinar?

To share your screen with other participants, click on the green icon which says **Share Screen** at the bottom of the main window.

A window like this will appear.

When this window pops up, you can choose the desktop or screen that you want to share with others. As soon as you click on **Share**, a window saying 'Allow Zoom to share your screen' will pop up. Click on **Open System Preferences** and select **Zoom** from the list.

Sharing the Zoom Screen and Pause Sharing

You can pause the screen by pressing the **Pause** button when you do not want the attendees watching you shuffle the presentation slides.

Share and Comment on Your Mobile Phone

You can share files directly from your phone while you are in a meeting, and use your phone's tablet function by typing notes with your finger. To make notes while viewing someone else's danger screen, click **Show Settings** at the top of the Zoom window, and then click **Notes**. A toolbar appears with all the options of markup, such as text, drawing, arrows, and so on.

Video Tutorial

Take the time in your first class to introduce Zoom to your students and make sure they can combine audio and video.

Enter a schedule for each category, by sharing a document or sliding it with screen sharing at the beginning of time. This gives students a clear picture of what the class is doing, what is being discussed, and what activities they are participating in.

Discuss online ethics and student expectations for the first virtual classroom and regularly review topics.

Use a spreadsheet or commentary on a shared document and allow students to commit. When you share a tape, document, screen, or image, test the math problems on the table or ask the student to use notes to highlight material on the paper to share, such as grammar errors.

Take the time to present your questions, comments, and feedback in class. Allow students to use feedback, write their questions in a chat, or shut them up to ask their questions live.

Divide them into smaller groups to discuss specific topics. You can use Zoom's **Breakout Rooms**, either in advance to assign, or automatically assign cars to groups for a short time so they can talk together.

We have seen screen sharing as one of the most interesting features of Zoom. Now I am going to detail where its high educational potential lies.

1. Group Classes

Sessions can host as many participants as if you were in the classroom. You can see and hear the students. You can see their faces as you explain, so you know if they are following you or are in the Yupi worlds.

2. Live Classes

Giving live sessions is something unmatched. Students are connected and share the virtual classroom with their classmates. A camaraderie and a feeling of closeness are generated despite the distance.

3. Deferred Classes

If any student is unable to attend live, you can see the recording of the class. Also, if the teacher can't give the class for whatever reason, you can record it earlier and have it play when the time comes.

4. Tutoring

It is a close and direct way to have a tutorial with each of your students. Audiovisual communication lowers barriers and helps to empathize with a much more natural way of communicating than a phone call.

5. Share Presentations

It is excellent and demands utility for every self-respecting teacher. What would a virtual class be without its PowerPoint or PDF presentation? You can also share the screen to show a photo or an exercise.

6. Share Videos

The possibility of screen sharing opens up a range of possibilities, among which the sharing of audiovisual content such as an interview with an expert in a certain subject, a documentary, or an educational video is included.

7. Virtual Whiteboard

This functionality allows us to turn our screen into a whiteboard. The advantage is that here there is no chalk to stain you and that erasing the board is a matter of clicking. It is very useful to solve exercises and make explanations with graphic support.

8. Raise Your Hand

The student can raise his hand as if it were a face-to-face class. The teacher will receive a rather subtle warning on their screen. In this way, you will know that there is a student who has a question and who it is. You can continue with your explanation or stop to solve it.

9. Create Surveys

A very cool feature to make the lesson more enjoyable and participatory is that the trainer can ask questions so that the students answer and validate their knowledge.

10. Chat

This is a very interesting functionality and a double-edged sword. It is interesting because it increases the interaction within the whole classroom; it is dangerous if a private chat is activated since students will be able to write to each other without the teacher knowing it and they will be distracted.

Chapter 9: How Do I Schedule A Recurring Webinar?

Zoom Video Webinar enables you to transmit up to ten thousands of view-only participants of a Zoom conference, based on the extent of your webinar permit. Webinar licenses begin at a capacity of a hundred participants and have a scale of up to ten thousand. You can display your computer, photo, and audio as the host or panel member in a webinar, and guests may use the talk or question and answer tools to connect with the moderator and panel members.

Pre-registration for Webinars

Webinars may involve pre-registration corresponding to the meeting. The host may either accept all registrants immediately or authorize them manually. The host will add queries regarding personalized registration, and remove the registration files. Optionally the webinar access may be switched off by the server. After entering, the passengers would also be asked to type their name and email address, and the records should be restricted to this.

Registration Approval Methods

There are two webinar acceptance forms, which include

registration.

1. **Approve Immediately:** All webinar account holders should instantly obtain a confirmation email containing information about how to access the webinar.

2. **Manually Accept:** The Webinar host must manually authorize or deny the consent of a registrant. If a registered owner is accepted, an email with instructions about how to access the webinar will be sent to them.

Schedule Webinar

1. Log in to the online server for the Zoom.

2. Select Webinars. The collection of planned webinars can be found here.

3. Choose a Webinar to Plan.

4. Use the webinar settings you need. Choose the date, time zone, topic, webinar password, and other registration settings.

5. Click to schedule the webinar.

Sending Invites

There are three forms to invite the participants to sign up:

1. Copy and distribute the Login URL via address, the websites, etc.

2. Click **Download the Invitation** to show and send the email or link that Zoom has generated to hand out to the participants.

3. Use your email to ask to obtain a copy of the invitation to Zoom, which you will then forward to future attendees.

Automatically Scheduled Meetings

Whenever someone at a scheduling program books a scheduled appointment, Zapier can produce a new Zoom assembly and insert it. With all those programs you use, below are a few Zaps to electricity this particular workflow. However, you can produce a Zap. You can add them to make this automation a stronger measure that shares the assembly details along with your group by means of a program like Slack. This automation is used all of the time by us at Zapier; the Zoom connection has posted to the station in Slack.

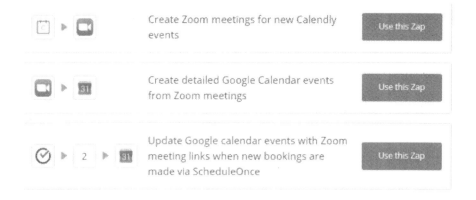

Create Zoom meetings for new Calendly events — Use this Zap

Create detailed Google Calendar events from Zoom meetings — Use this Zap

Update Google calendar events with Zoom meeting links when new bookings are made via ScheduleOnce — Use this Zap

Produce Recurring Meetings with Stored Configurations and Yet Another URL

For others, along with Zoom meetings, calls allow you to make a meeting. There are two advantages to using this particular setting. It permits you to have them, and also lock the call settings you need. Secondly, the same URL is used every time by recurring calls, which means you do not ever need to send one. Furthermore, if you match the identical group frequently although not on a normal program, you may go for an alternative, known as **No Fixed Time**, which permits you to use exactly the very same settings and assembly ID over and over using the identical group, regardless of when you purchase together. This option is popular with classes using Zoom as their classroom. The way you do that will depend on which stage you are using, but you also can consult with the documentation of Zoom for setting up your assembly. It is a fair warning that for any recurring meeting, you can't schedule it together with your **Private Meeting ID** (also known as PMI in Zoom; it is a digital private meeting area for you, where the connection never changes). Know that those meeting IDs die after one year, and that means you're going to need to create a new one.

Chapter 10: How Do I Set Up Meeting Breakout Rooms And Create A Waiting Room?

Breakout Rooms

You can split a larger meeting or classroom into smaller groups in Zoom.

Firstly, you have to enable the feature. Login to your account on your browser, click on the **Settings** tab, under **In Meeting (Advanced)**, scroll down and locate the **Breakout Room** option.

After you have activated this feature, as a host or co-host, you will have access to the **Breakout Rooms** feature. Open your Zoom software and click on the **Breakout Rooms** icon.

Now, to group the meeting into a smaller section, click on the **Breakout Rooms** icon and you will get a pop-up window asking you to assign participants into rooms.

Assigning participants into rooms can be done automatically

or manually.

Automatically, it will generate the breakout rooms itself. You can still go ahead and exchange one participant with another, as you wish.

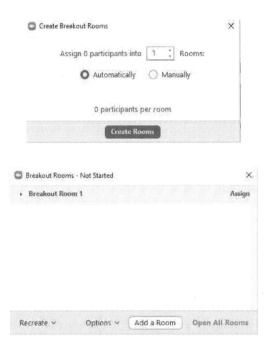

Once you are ready to open the rooms, click on **Open All Rooms** and your participants will be able to join the section that you have created for them.

As a host or co-host, you can go to different rooms to talk to the participants by using the **Join** button in each room.

You can also broadcast messages to everyone like '*One more minute to go*' (if you had given them classwork).

After the session, click on **Close All Rooms**, and they will be given a minute timer to rejoin the meeting.

You will notice that you still have the opportunity to reopen the rooms again, which is cool if you have a long session; you can create the group as often as you like.

Additionally, we have the option to close the breakout rooms after a specified amount of time. You can also change the timer.

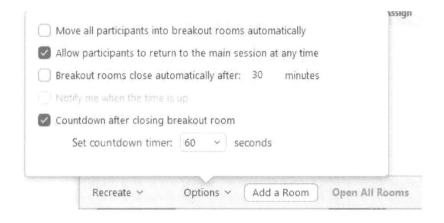

Virtual Waiting Room

This is a virtual queue where people will be attended to, one after another. The cool thing here is that people in the queue do not know who else is in the queue. This is really good for educators, counselors, consultants and others in the health care sector.

As a host, you can admit people in one after another,

remove them after their session and then admit the next person.

To create a virtual waiting room, you firstly schedule a meeting by clicking on **Schedule Meeting,** then fill in the basic requirements like the topic, duration, and so on.

Now click on the **Settings** tab, click on **In Meeting (Advanced)**, and scroll down to the **Waiting Room**, and then enable the feature.

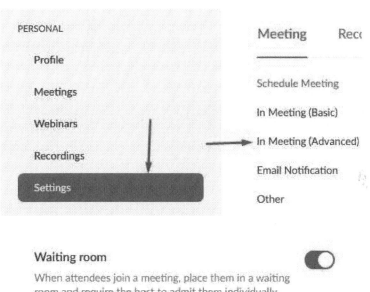

Also, make sure that **Join before Host** is disabled because you have to be the first person in your meeting.

That can be found here; Settings > Schedule Meeting > Scroll down to locate **Join before host.**

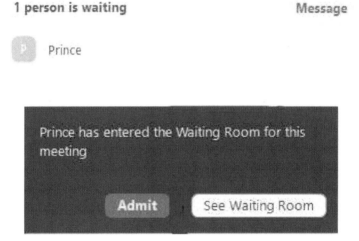

Then, you can go ahead and send your invitation link out to your participants.

You can now start your meeting while you admit one after another, whoever is in the waiting room.

Once you are done with a participant, you can just remove the participant by clicking on **More** beside the participant's name, and select **Remove.**

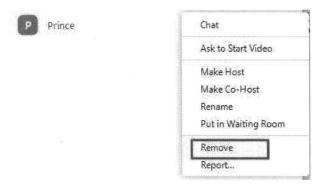

Then, you can admit the next participant in the waiting room.

Chapter 11: Can I Host and Join Meetings on a Mobile Device?

Telephone Zoom

Zoom Phone uses VoIP (Voice over Internet Protocol) to make Zoom calls through the cloud. This is similar to calling from a phone number, except that calls are hosted over the Internet here.

The Zoom Phone has many additional features that make your calling experience perfect.

These include:

- Integration with CRM as a sales representative

- Conference calls and delegation

- Call recording and voicemail functions

However, Zoom Phone is not available with the standard pricing plans. Instead, you have to pay separately. The pricing starts at $ 10 per user per month and requires that you have at least one licensed paid host.

Joining a Meeting via Telephone

You'll be provided with dial-in numbers for different

locations in the mail, inviting you to the meeting.

Identify your country of residence by the appropriate number.

Dial the number.

Remember your phone company may charge additional charges for these calls.

Android

Launch the app. You can also obtain the app on your play store.

You can participate in the interaction with any of the steps below:

1. Select **Join** to participate without your login details.

2. Log in with your information and select **Join**.

3. Input your identity digits and name.

4. If you log in, modify your name.

5. If you did not log in, input a name.

6. Click on **Attach files**, such as videos, and select **Join**.

iOS

Launch the platform app, and if you are yet to get the file, you should get it from the store.

You can participate in the interaction with any of the below concepts:

1. Select **Join** to gain access without login details.

2. Log into the application and select **Join**.

3. Input your identity digits and name.

4. If you log in with your details, modify your name.

5. If you did not log in, input a name.

6. Click on the attached materials and select **Join**.

Schedule a Meeting

Android

Launch the platform app and sign in.

Click on **Schedule**.

Choose your preferred interaction options. Few options will be unavailable because hosts may disable them, or set limits to the account grade and level.

1. **Topic**: Input a title for your video conversations.

2. Select your desired time for the project.

3. **Time Zone**: The platform utilizes the device time zone automatically. Select the menu that drops down to choose another zone.

4. **Repeat**: You can decide on a continuous conversation with the same identity for every program.

5. **Utilize Identity**: You should check this option if you wish to utilize your identity. But if the reverse is the case, it will generate a random identity.

6. To turn the host video **OFF** or **ON** while participating in the interaction, select the buttons respectively. If you select **OFF**, it will give the host the option of starting the video.

iOS

Launch the platform app on your gadget.

Select **Schedule**.

Tap **Options**. Few options will be unavailable because hosts may disable them or set limits to the account grade and level.

1. **Topic:** Input a title for your video conversations.

2. **Start**: Select a time for the project. You can begin any time before the time you have set for the program.

3. **Time Span**: Select the right time frame for the project. It will ensure that the interaction continues until the set time.

4. **Time Zone**: The platform utilizes the device time automatically. Select the menu that drops down to pick another zone.

5. **Repeat**: You can decide if you want a continuous conversation with the same identity for every program.

6. **Utilize Identity**: You should check this option if you wish to utilize your identity. But if the reverse is the case, it will generate a random identity.

7. **Audio Option**: You can decide if you want participants to call through their gadget's audio or the telephone. You can also utilize both.

Chapter 12: How Can I Prevent Zoom-Bombing from Happening?

What Is Zoom Bombing?

You have probably heard the term 'zoom-bombing' previously. This applies to people who are not invited, to obtain entry to Zoom calls and strive to cause havoc. There was a multitude of extensively confirmed incidents of zoom-bombing pretty recently, which led the organization to crack them down.

Increasing usability of the Zoom has led to abuse of the service by internet trolls and people who have too much time in their hands. Some people have searched for allotments and insecure ones, and then 'blasted' other people into the ring with videos, pornography, and other inappropriate content.

Instead, it will, by default, be password-protected once you initiate a call, making it tougher for someone you do not know to get connected to you. Many calls often have a **Waiting Room** feature, requiring the host to allow whoever wishes to access the call.

Because of their recent upgrade, all of the zoom users enjoy security coverage that helps them scale these threats.

Zoom-bombing/Zoom Raiding: It is an unwanted intrusion by hackers into a video conference.

Zoom was initially planned to be utilized in business settings, where most people attempt their best to act professionally. That is the reason it is extremely significant for the teachers/host to know the best settings and highlights to use to learn and limit the disturbance.

Here are a couple of key settings for keeping harmony in class.

Follow These Steps to Prevent Zoom Bombing As a Host

Zoom bombings are the result of the penetration of any uninvited user within the meeting with the intention of interrupting the meeting or ruining it. At times, users can enter a meeting accidentally. If the meeting is important or concerns professional business, it is necessary to prevent Zoom-bombing.

Create a Zoom meeting and prepare a password by tapping on **Require Meeting Password** under the **Password** section. Create a strong password and share it with the participants who are scheduled for the meeting. Any user without a password will be unable to join the meeting.

If you are using the **Waiting Room** feature, you can let the participants in one by one. To enable this feature, tap on **Advanced Settings** after signing in and check the **Enable Waiting Room** box.

If you do not want any of your participants to share the screen, tap on **Advanced Sharing Options** after clicking on the arrow beside **Share Screen**. You will be shown these questions, '*How many participants can share at the same time?*' And '*Who can share?*' For the former, select **One Participant Can Share at a Time** and for the other question, select **Only Host.**

Finally, go to **Manage Participants** in the Zoom toolbar (which shows all the active participants in the meeting) and click on **More** (located at the bottom right-hand part). Click on **Lock Meeting**. By selecting this option, all users out of this room will be barred from entering, even if they are provided with the password of the meeting.

Zoom Security Tips and How to Prevent Bombing

As a rule of thumb, when you share your meeting link on social media or other public forums, that makes your event extremely public, as anyone with the link can join in on your meeting, even if the person was not expressly invited. Keep your meeting links within your circles.

Zoom advises its users to avoid using their Meeting ID (PMI) to host public events. There is the option to generate random meeting IDs that one can use to host public events. The reason is simple; seeing that your PMI does not change unless you change it, using it to host public events only broadens the scale of uninvited people who can Zoom-bomb you, and that could be very annoying, as you can imagine. Your PMI should only be used to host meetings between you and other personal contacts who you allow to contact you.

Zoom has also made it easy to handle your meetings and protect them when they happen.

There are various security options that you can now access with a few taps. This includes the ability to lock the session when it begins so that no new people can enter, delete current call participants, mutate participants, and also disable private chat. To access the Zoom security tools, you can click the security button that appears in the window when the call occurs, or swing over a participant to interact with them specifically, for example, to remove them from the request.

- **Reporting Other Participants**

It is now feasible to report those participants on call who are not invited, or who cause trouble. Along with removing them from the call, you can now send a report to the **Zoom**

Confidence and Safety team to deal with device misuse. In the future, this would help block them from the service, and also interfere with other calls.

- **Password Protect Your Meetings**

Setting a password for your meeting is the easiest way to avoid unwanted attendances and hijacking. For all sessions, passwords can be placed at the individual encounter, user, party, or account level. To do so, first, log in to the Zoom web portal with your password. If you aim to create a password for the meeting at a single stage, go straight to the **Settings** tab and allow **Require a Password When Scheduling New Meetings** to ensure that when a meeting is scheduled, a password will be created. To enter the meeting, all participants need a password. Subscription holders may also opt to move to **Community Control** or allow everyone to follow the same password practices.

- **Authenticate Users**

Only require signed-in users to participate when creating a new event, if you want to.

- **Attend Before Host**

Do not encourage anyone to attend a meeting that has arrived before you, as the host. This setting can be applied to a party under **Account Settings**.

- ## Set a Password for the Conference

Setting a password will allow you to control who joins the conference and prevent uninvited guests from participating. You need to activate this setting on the Zoom website under Account Management> Settings> Conference (tab)> At Conference (basic).

- ## Make Sure That Only the Organizer Can Share His Screen with Other Participants

Do not let others capture the screen during the conference. To do this, make sure that your settings indicate that the only people who are allowed to share their screens are meeting organizers. You can enable this setting, both in advance on the Zoom website under *Account Management> Settings> Conference (tab)> At Conference (basic),* and during a conversation.

- ## Block Access to The Conference After It Starts

If you start a conference, and all the invitees have already joined it, you can block the meeting from new participants. During the meeting, click the **Manage Participants** button at the bottom of the interface. The **Participants Panel** will open. At the bottom of the screen, select the conference *Lock* option.

- ## Unplug Someone's Camera or Microphone

Organizers can mute any participant's camera or microphone. If someone behaves rudely or inappropriately through the camera, or his video has some technical problem, the presenter can open the **Participant Management Panel**, and click on the video camera icon next to the person's name. In the same place at the bottom of the panel, you can turn off the sound for all participants in the Zoom-conference.

- ## Disable Private Chat

If you invite strangers to join the call, one of the participants may send unwanted private messages to other participants. Or people may start discussing you behind your back. You can prevent this by disabling the private chat feature. Disabling private chat does not affect the public chat, which all participants in the conversation can see and participate in the conversation.

- ## Switch in Participants-Screen Sharing

No one wants to see obscene material shared by a Zoom bomber, and so it is worthwhile disabling the capacity of the participants to share their images. This choice can be accessed inactive sessions through the new **Security** tab.

- ## Use a Randomly Generated ID

Whenever possible, you should not use your meeting ID because this might pave the way for pranksters or attackers who know how to interrupt online sessions. Alternatively, when creating a new event, choose a randomly generated ID for meetings. Besides, you will not publicly display your ID.

- **Using Waiting Rooms**

The **Waiting Room** feature is a way of screening guests before they can join a meeting. Although genuinely useful for purposes such as interviews or virtual office hours, this also allows hosts more control over the security of the session.

- **Avoid File Sharing**

Be careful with the meeting's file sharing function, particularly if users you do not know send content across, as it may be malicious.

Instead, use a trusted service like Box or Google Drive to share the content. Zoom has disabled this function anyway at the time of writing because of potential vulnerability to protection.

- **Remove Nuisance Attendees**

You can kick them out under the **Participants** tab if you think anyone is disturbing a meeting. Select **More** over the titles and delete them. Additionally, by disabling **Allow excluded participants to participate** under the tab *Settings> Meetings> Standard*, you will make sure they cannot participate.

- **Check for Updates**

As security problems occur and fixes are implemented, or functions are disabled, make sure you have the new construction. To search, open the desktop program, click in the top-right of your profile, and pick **Search for Updates**.

Chapter 13: Should I Record My Webinar Locally or to the Cloud? How to Do It?

Recording Meetings

This depends on the account that you are using; a paid account gives you the opportunity of saving all your recordings either locally, or on the cloud. This singular act makes it possible for even those that are present at the time of the meeting, to be able to have a view of what actually transpired. However, if you are operating on a free account, the only option you have is to save the audio or the recordings locally on the computer. Lectures, introductions, guest visitors, screencasts, and anything can be made the easiest with the aid of the capability of Zoom.

- To commence the recording of a meeting, there is a **Record** button to be clicked on the toolbar.

- And then, on the top right corner of the screen, there is an indicator for the recording that will be displayed as soon as the recording begins.

- On the toolbar, there is a button to **pause** or **stop** the recording, and also at the top of the page is a pause icon that will be used to stop or pause the recording when desired.

Note this about free accounts:

It is possible not to see the record button at the top right corner if one is operating on a free account. Here are some of the simple steps to follow in order to rectify that.

Firstly, log out of the account if it was logged to the application on the desktop.

Navigate to *https://www.zoom.us,* and log in to the account. Then click the **Sign Up** option on the right top corner present in the window. As soon as this is achieved, enter your password along with the email address, and then press the **Sign in** button. Then next thing to do is to check the menu to the left of the screen, and then to check the meeting settings. Over the area is a recording link, or a tab to be followed for direction. To turn it **ON**, toggle local recording, and that is all that is left for you to start recording. If it prompted **Turn on Again**, it should be clicked, and you can now log back to the computer. There will appear the record button this time.

How to Record Meetings on Your Mobile Phone

Call and conference calls can also be recorded on a mobile phone. However, this is done with cloud recordings, so you will need to pay to use this feature. It is paramount that cloud storage is limited, so please note how many meetings you enter via the mobile software.

Follow these steps to record a zoom call on your mobile phone:

1. Open the zoom app on your mobile phone.

2. Click to **Join** or start a meeting.

3. Click on the three-point menu in the lower-right corner of the screen.

4. Click **Save to the cloud** or **Save**.

5. You will then see the **Save** icon and the option to **Pause** or **Stop Recording**.

6. When the call is completed, you can find the recording in the **My Recordings** section of the Zoom web page.

How to Use Virtual Backgrounds in Mobile Apps

You can also use virtual backgrounds from Zoom in the app.

Log in to your account and join the conference call. Then click on the three boxes at the bottom of the screen and click the **Add** menu. Then click on **Virtual Background** and select the background to use.

Edit Background Appearance

In addition to the virtual foundation, Zoom also offers the opportunity to enhance your look during a call. There is an operation called 'Touch Your Looks' which is useful if you have not received a daily caffeine fix or if you are struggling with life in your office.

Touch your look with the filter to optimize fine lines as it is designed to look very natural. To use my touchscreen, go to **Settings** and select the **touchscreen** for touching on the Video tab.

How to Record Straight to iCloud

In addition to recording Zoom meetings, you can also automatically copy the audio of the meeting you are recording to the cloud. And as meeting guests, you can edit the text, scan the text of your keywords to make the video happen at that moment, and share the recording.

To permit the audio file operation for your use, visit the Zoom portal and proceed to the **Meeting Settings,** then **Cloud Storage** on the recording tab, and affirm that the setting is allowed. Click **Apply** if salient. Once the option is gray, it will be under the key sign at either the group, or account level, and you must call your Zoom Manager.

Zoom Gallery

Viewing the presentation, 49 participants in the meeting can be seen, not the default 25, though it counts on the device.

The distinguished Zoom software on Android and iOS permits you to start or join a meeting. As it comes, the Zoom application's Zoom screen is visible over the active speaker. When more participants are entering the meeting, you will see a thumbnail of a video in the lower right corner. You can watch videos from up to four participants at a time.

Zoom allows macOS or Windows to view 49 people. When the desktop application is installed on your computer, go to **Settings**, and click **Video** to display the **Video Settings** page. Then proceed with the option **Showcase up To 49 Participants in a Box View** setting.

Chapter 14: Easy Strategies to Make Your Class More Fun and Engaging

The transition from physical classes to virtual learning could be a daunting task. It is not uncommon for teachers to struggle with getting started. The following are a few helpful ideas to implement. First, set aside a familiar place from which to teach. Students attest to the familiarity of the classroom in aiding with the ease of learning as well as recollection during tests and exams. Teachers should select a spacious, well lit, and comfortable spot and decorate it, as close as possible, to your physical classroom. Supplying the area with all of the equipment and resources needed for each class is a must. This personal teaching environment will go a long way in ensuring proper communication, organization, and classroom management.

Creating student independence and responsibility regarding their own learning is by all accounts, perhaps, the best thing you can do to prepare your students for autonomy. Student autonomy, in any case, should be understood as a process instead of a state. It is frequently mistaken for empowering self-guidance, and this could absolutely be one of the results, yet the concept goes beyond that. By assuming responsibility for their learning, your students will turn out to be able to engage better in the class, try out more difficult projects, and learn better. In addition, it should help with boosting their innate motivation, as they find their own voice.

The establishment of a classroom website or portal to serve as a resource hub is also recommended when beginning an online teaching experience.

According to Mertens (2008), a resource hub should have sources of information both in print and in an audio-visual form. It should serve to encourage self-instruction (independent or supervised) and provide for individual or group work (Mertens, 2008). Prior to the COVID-19 pandemic, students alternated between classes, teachers, buildings, labs, etc. This new era, with an emphasis on e-learning, requires a method to incorporate them all. Building a classroom website places all the necessary resources in one place. Students should be able to get all materials needed for learning via this website. Links to other relevant sites, research publications, and textbooks, videos, and other related resources should all be accessible via the classroom website. This gives students confidence that their needs and convenience have been considered which should lessen any virtual learning apprehensions that may exist.

Virtually Unprecedented

Now that virtual education has become the order of the day, teachers need to be aware of the limitless resources available online. These include resources on how to make the best of teaching in a virtual world, setting up a virtual teaching environment, organizing materials for students, and setting assessments for them. There is virtually no 'how-to' that the internet has not tackled. This makes teaching for e-learning easier to take on. It is to the advantage of any instructor to make the best use of these resources prior to, during, and after virtual classes have been started. Likewise, establishing and maintaining a bank of resources that are 'content area' and 'grades level' specific, will save time when planning lessons, employing supplemental materials, differentiating instructions, accelerating learning, and re-teaching.

Pre-course evaluation is important when starting an online class.

Teachers should prepare a pretest that students can take before the instruction starts. This is to assess their prior knowledge of the course content and to inform them of what standards and learning points are expected to be reached over the course of the study, and by the end of the course. The results will also serve as baseline data for progress, monitoring student learning, and achievement going forwards after formative assessments are administered and scored.

Johnson 2017 identified six key tactics for creating impactful virtual learning environments. The first tactic entails dividing learning activities into short, video-based modules. The second tact is to build 'extracurricular learning' paths followed by promoting employee collaboration and ideation. Gamification is yet another tactic. Additionally, encouraging employee feedback and facilitating new skill development offerings, internally rounds out the list.

Gamification: The Power of Learning by Playing

The main goal of teachers is to motivate their pupils to learn because learning often depends on the composition of heterogeneous classes. These include both capable students to activate effective learning strategies, and using knowledge already well acquired, and not to be discouraged in the face of difficulties. Students should not process the contents superficially, have the strength to persist in the face of obstacles, and show confidence in their ability. In an educational context of pupils with these characteristics, teachers are inevitably faced with severe educational challenges. It, moreover, puts in crisis the teaching scheme today, based on sequence explanation, individual study, and written and oral verification. Through games, we try to structure learning by examining a psychological construct of great interest and educational relevance, such as motivation to learn through play. Currently, there has been a rediscovery of games as an activity that is considered to be important. The games have recently aroused interest in the world (related to training in the company, in management, and school) as a support to the cognitive and educational processes. Only recently, this interest has known an exceptional thrust and found appropriate practical formulations. Today, the theme of the game and its use in educational contexts has assumed the semblance of gamification.

Responding appropriately is becoming increasingly

important and indispensable. It is because an increasing number of organizations, among the most advanced ones, are introducing gamification-based applications because the phenomenon has the potential to revolutionize in many ways the way you learn, work, communicate, and do business. The inevitable consequence is an inflated use of the term and often is used as a real abuse, which threatens to lead it to empty its intrinsic meaning gradually. That's why you want to start the journey inside the world of gamification, through answers to previously defined key concepts that will serve to clear doubts and misunderstandings about this phenomenon.

Games have accompanied the history of man in the millennia, is well-known, and is an intensely studied theme.

Gamification is a term not entirely transparent, is partly controversial, and is understood with a variety of accents derived from game, so it has to do with the idea of play. Gamification can, therefore, be represented as a kind of 'substrate,' which is a level made of rules and strategies typical of the playful world (called a 'game mechanic' or 'game technique'). We can superimpose and apply it to the other worlds, such as that of learning, training, or marketing.

Even when teaching online, it is essential to create a classroom environment with which students want to interact. Live lesson sessions through the use of technology can help create a classroom environment. Using excellent visual aids can help students find fun and joy in their learning. As a teacher, you can even use technology to record fun videos or organize live lesson sessions or individual conversations so that students can interact with you in real-time. Students want and need such interactions with a teacher so that they can trust and learn well from them.

Call students by their names, remember any kind of detail about them and create stories during the different lessons to help you create a fun and comfortable classroom environment. Online teaching is becoming increasingly popular today, and teachers are expected to go beyond their comfort zone to reach students. Technology is extremely helpful in helping teachers create meaningful learning environments within an online session.

Smart Ways to Engage Your Online Students

You, as a teacher, should be able to anticipate and address problems by implementing the following strategies to keep students engaged.

Regularly Update the Course Content

Why not do some research and development on various current affairs that might be of interest to students? The Internet is full of resources or lesson plans based on the latest developments. There are many online sources of information, such as news websites, articles, videos, podcasts, and conference session recordings. As a course designer, you could also incorporate recent policies, regulations, or various reviews.

Whatever you choose as your course content, it is always a great idea to take into account all the latest trends as well as the emerging practices from various sectors.

Assign Successful Coaches

At many colleges and universities, successful coaches are assigned to students who attend online courses. These individuals provide tips on learning and studying online, as well as offer assets to assist students in dealing with tasks and managing time. A learning coach (you could actually choose what you will call such a person) also helps students identify or plan their learning path, by directing students to external resources.

The added value of successful coaches is significant, since they take the online learning program to the next level.

Coaches can also help students reach specific course milestones, and avert any sidetracking or distractions.

Encourage Responsibility

There are some easy tweaks that you can make in order to follow up on students. If you have a learning management system (LMS), there is no need to worry. There are a number of tools, such as **Remind**, which allows instant, yet safe communication among educators, parents and teachers.

The key point is to show students that they are not alone and ignored throughout this learning process. Such tools also allow for receiving comments or any kind of communication.

Small Teaching Online Quick Tip: Creating Autonomy

Here are some ways to create autonomy particularly through online discussions:

1. **Request That Your Students Help Shape Conversation Necessities**

Your prospectus should show the significance of conversations in your online course and the learning goals they line up with. You could ask your students to offer feedback on this part of the learning plan, and should permit them to contribute to what class conversations should look like and what the prerequisites will be.

2. Offer Choices in Conversation Prompts

Students are bound to dive deeper into their work (and find importance in it) when they are looking for the questions that interest them instead of the ones you have set for them. Another approach to promote student autonomy through your online conversations is to give your students different prompts to explore and ask that they react to one. Along these lines, your students would not feel compelled to discuss something they are not interested in, and they can recognize the material and thoughts that interest them the most.

3. Let Your Students Pick How to Answer

Move away from standard written answers and permit your students to take part in conversations by recording voice answers, video answers, or short audiovisual presentations.

4. **Give Your Students a Choice Between Simultaneous and On and Off Conversations**

While your simultaneous class groups probably won't be obligatory for online students, you could consider giving your students a choice between answering to conversations non-concurrently, and participating in a coordinated web conferencing meeting (e.g., Zoom). This is an incredible method to take into account students who like the spontaneity and natural nature of eye to eye conversations. You could also record the meeting and share it with the rest of the class afterward so nobody is left out of the learning opportunities these meetings give.

5. **Offer Alternative Options for Online Conversations**

Confer with your students, and find out if they are interested in elective techniques for connection. This could include something like teaming up on comments using a tool like **Hypothesis** or making a Google Doc of shared notes.

Being open to student contribution and how online conversations are driven, will help you in promoting student autonomy while urging students to connect with the course material and their classmates in important ways. By giving your students more choices in online conversations, you can move past the tedious 'I agree' responses to more thoughtful and deliberate conversations.

Chapter 15: 10 Zoom Tips & Tricks Every Teacher Must Know

The Zoom platform is an excellent answer to video interaction and communication problems faced by businesses and large organizations. The platform comprises of several essential attributes. It is, therefore, important to understand several tips and tricks of the program. Below are a few tricks that you should know to improve your experience.

1 Use Virtual Background

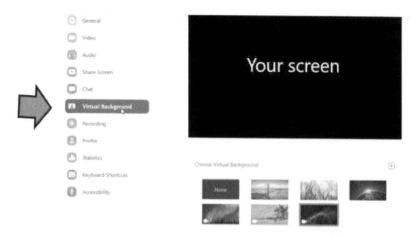

The platform consists of various attributes, but this is a wonderful one. It lets users attach a custom background to their project. It could be in the form of materials, like an image or video, in the course of the interaction. It also provides several out-of-the-box media, and users can include their video or picture to the background of their project.

The program can differentiate between the background and the face of the user in real-time. You must allow the feature if you want to utilize it. Select the **Cogswell** logo to launch the **Settings,** and navigate to the **Virtual Background**. In this section, you can decide what type of image you want as the virtual background. You can choose several available options.

2 Disallow Videos When You Want To Join a Video Interaction

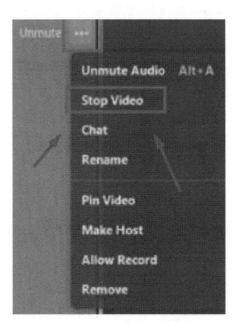

At some point in time, you might get a video alert and join the call quickly without preparation. The platform offers a solution to fix that problem. The **Disallow** feature can save you from that embarrassment. There is an option for you to disallow the feature permanently any time you want to link up with an interaction. Whenever you are fit enough to face the camera, you can turn it back on and utilize it. If you want to utilize this attribute, navigate to your settings, and launch it. Select the video and allow **Turn My Video Off** anytime you join a meeting.

3 Allow Gallery View

There are several attributes that the platform comprises, but you are going to love and admire this one. It keeps everyone on one page, and you keep track of all the attendants in the interaction in one place at the same time. You can also utilize this attribute anytime you put together small groups, and you must turn it on if you want to use it. To allow it, select **Gallery View**, and you can enjoy the outstanding experience it offers.

4 Automatically Copy Invitation URL

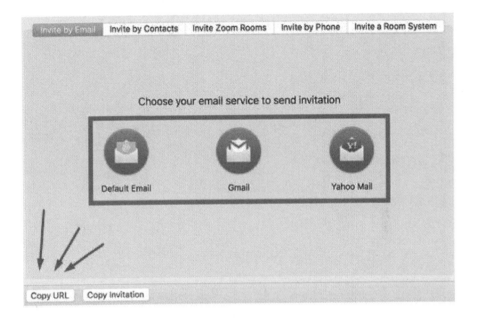

If you want to invite lots of attendants to your video interaction, you must utilize a global attribute that the platform offers, which you can utilize to copy the invitation URL and place it on your clipboard. You can save lots of time by selecting **Invite** and locating the URL for it. So launch the **Settings** and toggle **General**. Then allow **Automatically Copy the URL** anytime the interaction begins. You can start sending invites to attendants that you want to participate by distributing the link on social media and several platforms with ease.

5 Utilize Snap Camera

It is the desktop version of Snapchat that gives users the power to include several filters to beautify them from the application, so that they can build lenses. Users can distribute the lenses using the platform and set it as default. The attribute is a wonderful one that you will enjoy using, especially if you put together a group call to your relatives or friends.

If you want to utilize it, you need to get its app for the version of your device and select an image utilizing any of the available lenses. After performing that task, launch the app and navigate your way to **Settings**. Beneath the section for **Video**, modify the location of the camera from the menu that drops down to the **Snap Camera** feature.

6 Unify Third-Party Applications

The platform has compatibility with third-party apps that you can unify easily with one tap. If you want to participate in meetings through the platform, get the app from the store, and you are good to go. You can also utilize the feature to import the schedules you create for the interaction, through Outlook or the Calendar app from Google.

You can meet relatives and business partners on several platforms and begin interactions with only one click. You should know that you can find an app that can perform that function very well. You can locate every app that you require on the platform store.

7 Allow Records

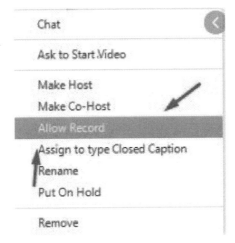

Another important trick that the platform can perform is recording conversations held by the entire group of people involved in the interaction. For example, you can record the interaction on your gadget by tapping the **record** control key while the interaction is in progress; it will begin.

The files of the conversation will be inside the **Documents** section. The platform can also provide recordings via the cloud, but only users of a certain age can utilize this feature; paid account-holders can enjoy this benefit.

8 Audio Transcript

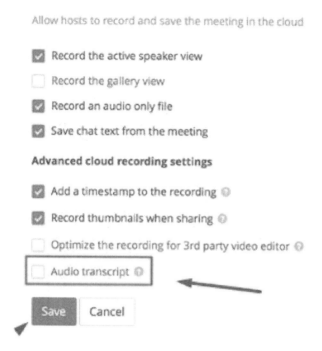

There is an important attribute that users can utilize to transcribe the audio recordings of an interaction, automatically. Users can use it to keep records and important parts of interactions inside a VTT text file. Only paid accounts that want to record via cloud have the opportunity to utilize this attribute.

If you have a paid account, you should launch the platform browser for recording and allow records for the cloud. Then, select **Advanced Settings** and check the box **Allow On the Audio Transcript**. Anytime you find yourself in an interaction, select **Record for Cloud** beneath the page. The platform will send an email after a few minutes, notifying you of the status of the transcript.

9 Stealth Mode

It is a wonderful attribute associated with the platform. It ensures that users gain access to video interactions with no sound. It is wonderful to utilize the access when the interaction is in progress and you want to avoid interruption at all costs. It is important to have a working device mic, though.

Launch the app and select **Settings**.

Tick the boxes you wish to include from the audio section, to mute the mic anytime you enter an integration beneath the visual display.

You can participate in an interaction without turning your video on, which is important for low bandwidth areas and locations with quality problems.

10 Emoji on Screen

If the host of an interaction mutes your account, you can display your reaction with the utilization of emojis. You can decide which to send; there are lots of available options, including the clapping emoji and the thumbs-up emoji. It is easy to communicate your feelings with emojis.

Whenever you want to use them in an interaction, select **Reactions** beneath the visual conversation display, and select your desired choice. It can disappear in less than ten seconds. If the interaction administrator allows the nonverbal response attribute, attendants can put a logo, like raising a finger, which indicates that they want to contribute to the interaction. Each individual in the group can see the replies to the emojis.

Conclusion

Although online learning has been around for many decades, the world had not appreciated its relevance until the moment that there was a global need for it. This has been the best time for us to adopt the existing flexible means of education that doesn't require the students and teachers to have physical contact before knowledge is imparted. By making use of the available resources online, our children can stay home during any period of isolation and enjoy their learning. Online learning can help to create a form of engagement with the students and prevent them from experiencing mental isolation.

This book remains a valuable guide that helps to show the way to keep our minds at work by using the Zoom technology as an alternative rather than giving ourselves to the hindrance caused by the situation around us. Hence, we need to prepare ourselves and note that there is always a way out, especially when it has to do with our children's education. Teachers will always have a means of carrying out their daily duties!

The future prospects for distance learning are limitless. Obviously, distance programs and classes are here to live, and will through in the future, but there are several unanswered things to be answered and investigated. While distance learning may be at least as effective in certain situations as conventional classroom learning, e-learning has not been claimed to be a replacement for conventional classroom instruction. Before learners join any distance learning program, they'd best make sure they looked closely at these things to make sure they got the education they wanted to meet your personal interests, your talents, and your career goals. The 21st-century teaching means the 21st generation teaching. It means supporting and controlling the learning of the students and implementing the skills of the 21st-century. Teachers must, therefore, be very pleased with any new technology to ensure the best virtual learning; classroom next to classroom physics Zoom offers a critical platform to encourage combined learning and career growth and to introduce Zoom.

The concept of education has recently changed from teacher to student. Previously, teachers took on the role of an information society, but their work has now expanded. There is a strong emphasis on integrating technology/innovation in the classroom, with intelligent teaching methods that focus on empowering students to achieve their chosen learning goals. Technology encourages greater student involvement, which is very important for achieving the desired learning objectives. Mixed learning allows students and teachers to make regular progress. It should be noted that the goal is not just to integrate technology into the classroom; moreover, educational objectives should define other teaching methods.

Now teachers can use different educational technologies like Zoom in combination with traditional classroom environments to improve student learning conditions.

Printed in Great Britain
by Amazon